Emma

ISBN: 1480170135
ISBN 13: 9781480170131

Illustration ideas from Julie Kim

For my Uncle Jung Rai Kim,
For my mother Soon Rae Kim,
For my grandmother Jung Ae Oh,
My three guardian angels;
My love and respect goes out
to you all.

For Stacey Kim,
My best friend, support and
confidante
For Helenmarieann Marconi,
My guide and confidante
For Donghwan Seo and
Jungmoo Heo,
My buddies and support

Emma loved to read.

So she read and read and read.

Emma loved reading to others.

So she read and read
and read to others.

Emma loved to think of stories.

So she thought and thought
and thought.

Emma loved to tell her stories.

So she told and told and told
her stories to others.

As Emma got older,
she loved to write.

So she wrote
and wrote and wrote.

Emma wrote about
the stories she thought of.

So she thought and wrote,
thought and wrote.

Then one day,
Emma published her stories
and became a writer.

From then on,
Emma continuously thought,
wrote, and told her stories
for others to read.

After reading the story, complete the activity pages that follow.

PAST AND PRESENT TENSE VERBS

Below, you will find four verbs written in the **present tense**. Write the **past tense** form of each verb next to the number. Example: 1) run-ran 2) hope-hoped 3) eat-ate 4) talk-talked

Present Tense Verbs   **Past Tense Verbs**

read   1}_____

think   2}_____

tell   3}_____

write   4}_____

Below are two **present tense** verbs. Can you write the **past tense** form of each verb?

BONUS

love   a}_____

become   b}_____

INFINITIVES

INFINITIVES = TO + A VERB

(Example: to + eat = to eat; "to others," found in the story, is not an infinitive because the word "others" is NOT a verb.)

Find the infinitives in the story.

1} P_____

2} _____

3} _____

4} _____

COMPARE AND CONTRAST

1

2

Take a look at picture one and picture two. How many similarities and differences can you find between the two pictures?

Similarities	Differences
1}_____	1}_____
_____	_____
_____	_____
2}_____	2}_____
_____	_____
_____	_____
3}_____	3}_____
_____	_____
_____	_____

1

2

Take a look at picture one and picture two. How many similarities and differences can you find between the two pictures?

Similarities	Differences
1}_____	1}_____
_____	_____
_____	_____
2}_____	2}_____
_____	_____
_____	_____
3}_____	3}_____
_____	_____
_____	_____

1

2

Take a look at picture one and picture two. How many similarities and differences can you find between the two pictures?

Similarities	Differences
1}_____	1}_____
_____	_____
_____	_____
2}_____	2}_____
_____	_____
_____	_____
3}_____	3}_____
_____	_____
_____	_____

Lessons for Teachers/Parents

Teachers and parents, grammar lessons can be taught using this book. For example, children and beginner/intermediate level of ESL students in all grade levels can learn the **past and present tense of regular verbs,** such as: **work/work<u>ed</u>, hope/hope<u>d</u> (just add a -d or -ed at the end of the verb to create the past form); and irregular verbs,** such as: **think/ thought, write/wrote, tell/told, rĕad/rēad (make sure to note the pronunciation differences from the present to the past with the word "read.")**

Secondly, a grammar lesson on infinitives can be taught.

An infinitive = to + a verb. It can start out simple for young children and beginning level of ESL students. For older children and intermediate/advanced level of ESL students, infinitives can become more complex when using them as **nouns, adjectives**, and **adverbs.** For example: To sleep is the only thing Emma wants after writing. To sleep **functions as a noun**

because it is the subject of the sentence. Another example: Emma wrote late into the night to complete her book. To complete **functions as an adverb because it explains why Emma wrote late into the night**. Using infinitives in different parts of speech make it more challenging for older children.

The simple present and past tense of regular verbs start out simple then become more complex using irregular verbs; thus, making this book useful for the various grades and English levels in schools and at home.

Finally, although repetition is not part of a grammar lesson, it is contained in the book for young elementary school children and beginning level of ESL students to practice reading and writing with. Words such as rĕad, thought, told, and wrote have been repeated in the story for that purpose.

This book will serve as a useful tool for teachers and parents in preparing a variety of fun and interesting grammar lessons as well as reading and writing practice.

Made in the USA
Charleston, SC
02 April 2013